My First German Book

LITTLE
VERBA

www.littleverba.co.uk

© 2025 Little Verba. Fiannova Ltd. All rights reserved.

THANK YOU FOR LEARNING WITH US!

WE WORK HARD TO MAKE SURE OUR TRANSLATIONS AND PRONUNCIATIONS ARE CLEAR AND ACCURATE FOR LITTLE LEARNERS

IF YOU SPOT ANYTHING THAT DOESN'T LOOK OR SOUND RIGHT, JUST LET US KNOW AT: HELLO@LITTLEVERBA.CO.UK

IF THE BOOK IS UPDATED, WE'LL HAPPILY SEND YOU A REPLACEMENT COPY

Around The Home

Im Haus
im hous

Lampe
lam-peh
lamp

Fenster
fen-ster
window

Bett
bet
bed

Stuhl
shtool
chair

Pflanze
flaan-tseh
plant

Schubladen
shoo-blah-den
drawers

Kitchen
Küche
koo-cheh

Kochtopf
kokh-topf
cooking pot

Tasse
tah-seh
cup

Teller
tel-ler
plate

Besteck
beh-shtek
cutlery

Glas
glahs
glass

Kühlschrank
kyool-shrank
fridge

Ofen
oh-fen
oven

It's Time To Go To Bed

wasch deine Hände
vash dy-neh hen-deh
wash your hands

Handseife
hant-zy-feh
hand soap

putz dir die Zähne
puts deer dee tsee-neh
brush your teeth

zieh deinen Schlafanzug an
tsee dy-nen shlahf-an-tsoog an
put on your pajamas

Zahnbürste
tsahn-byur-steh
toothbrush

Zahnpasta
tsahn-pah-stah
toothpaste

Es ist Zeit ins Bett zu gehen
es ist tsayt ins bet tsoo geh-en

vergiss den Teddy nicht
fair-giss den ted-dee nikht
don't forget teddy!

lies eine Gutenachtgeschichte
lees eye-neh goo-te-nakht-ge-shiḫ-teh
read a bedtime story

mach das Licht aus
makh das likht ous
turn out the light

sag gute Nacht
zahg goo-te nahḫt
say goodnight

Family and Relationships

Mutter
moo-ter
mother

Vater
fah-ter
father

Schwester
shves-ter
sister

Bruder
broo-der
brother

Cousin
koo-san
cousin

Baby
bay-bee
baby

Familie und Beziehungen
fah-mee-lee-eh oont beh-tsee-oong-en

Oma
oh-mah
grandma

Opa
oh-pah
grandad

Onkel
on-kel
uncle

Tante
tan-teh
aunt

Freunde
froy-nde
friends

Let's Play With Toys

Krankenschwester
kran-ken-shves-ter
nurse

Puppe
poo-peh
doll

Feuerwehrmann
foy-er-vehr-man
fireman

Verkleidung
fair-klai-doong
dressing up clothes

Bausteine
bow-shty-neh
blocks

Auto
ow-toh
car

Teddy
ted-dee
teddy

Lass uns mit Spielzeug spielen
las oons mit shpeel-tsoyk shpee-len

Puzzle
puh-zell
jigsaw puzzle

Welches Teil fehlt?
vel-khes tyle faylt
which is the missing piece?

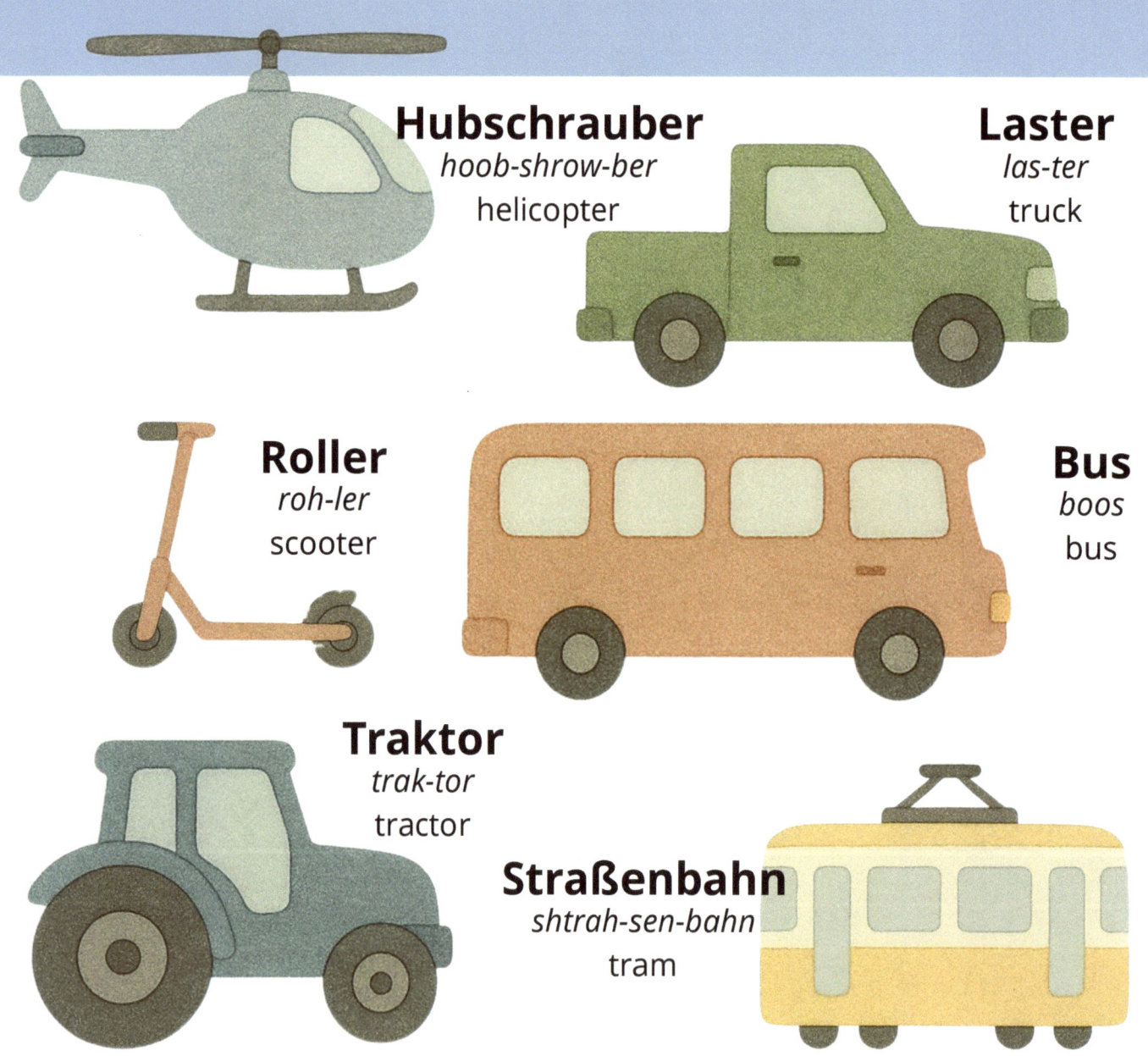

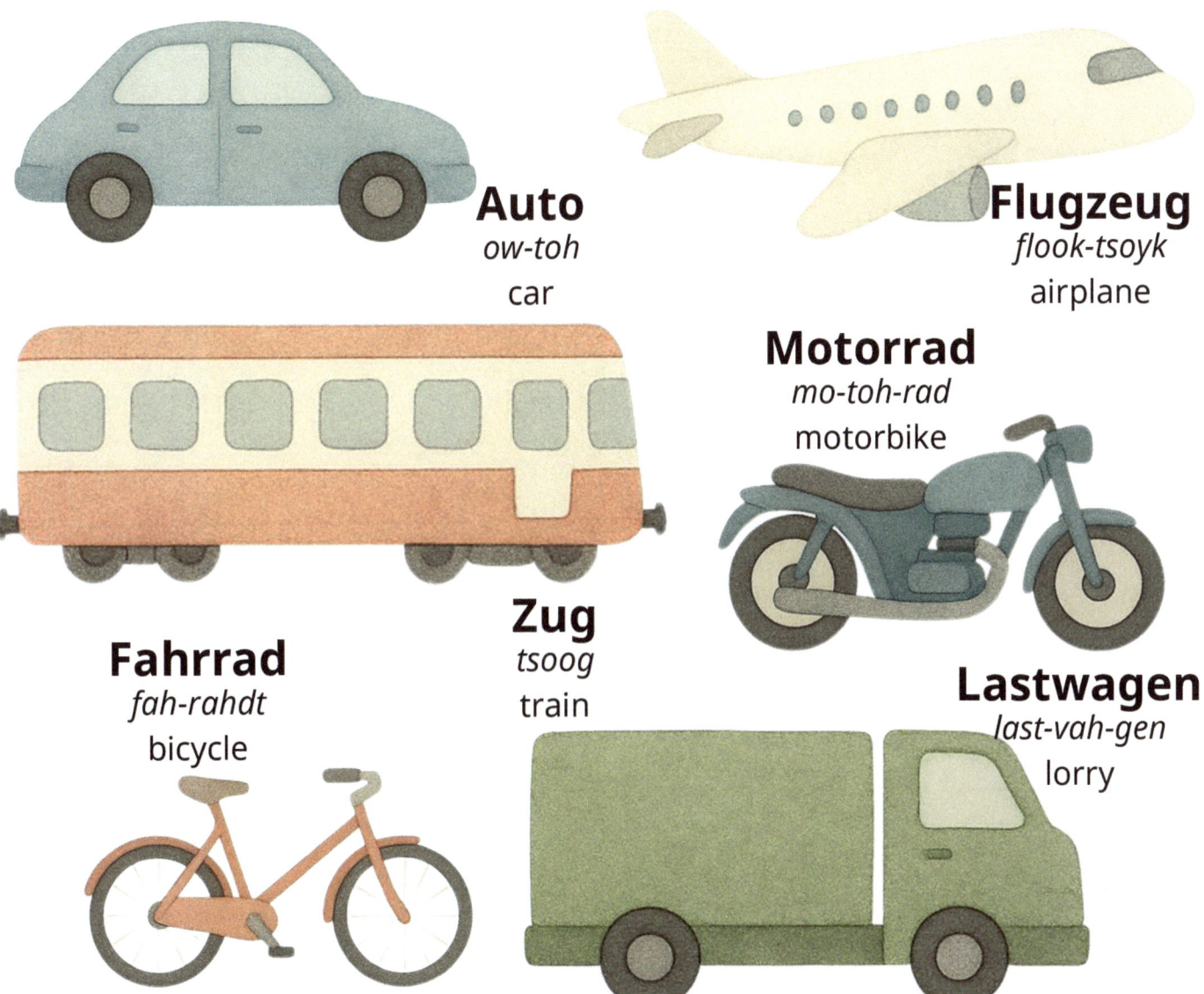

Wild Animals
Wildtiere
vilt-teer-eh

Löwe
lur-veh
lion

Pinguin
ping-gwheen
penguin

Giraffe
gee-rahf-feh
giraffe

Zebra
tseh-brah
zebra

Affe
ah-feh
monkey

Tiger
tee-ger
tiger

Jobs and Work Equipment

Arzt
ahrtst
doctor

Bauarbeiter
bow-ar-by-ter
builder

Koch
kohh
chef

Lehrer
lay-rer
teacher

Polizist
poh-lee-tsist
police officer

Postbote
post-boh-teh
postman

Actions and Senses

Handlungen und Sinne

hant-loong-en oont zin-neh

sehen
zay-en
seeing

riechen
ree-khen
smelling

hören
her-ren
hearing

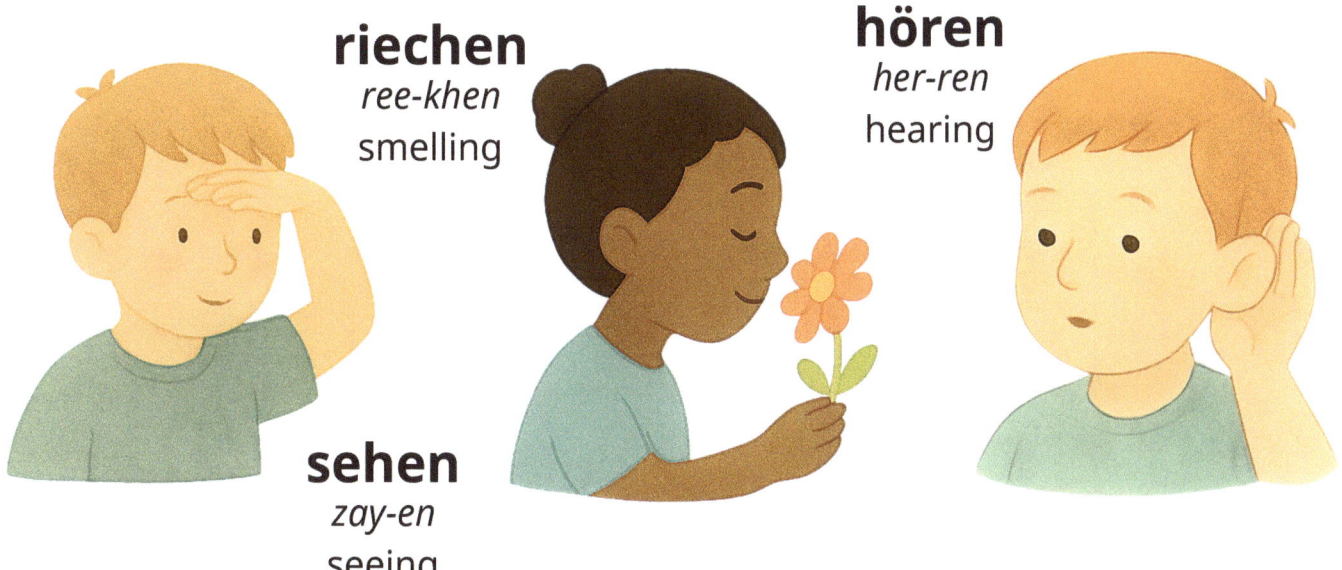

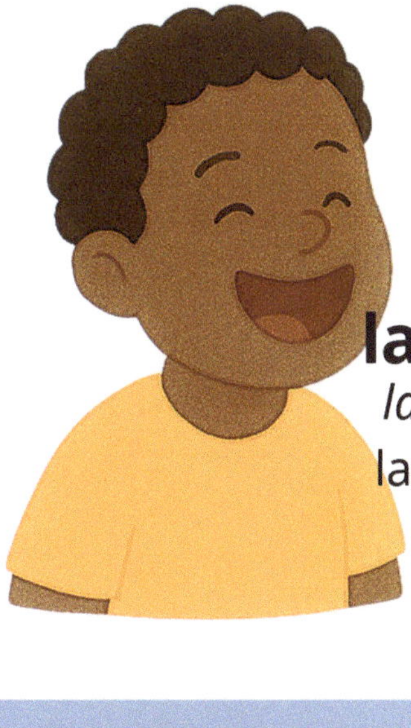

lachen
lah-khen
laughing

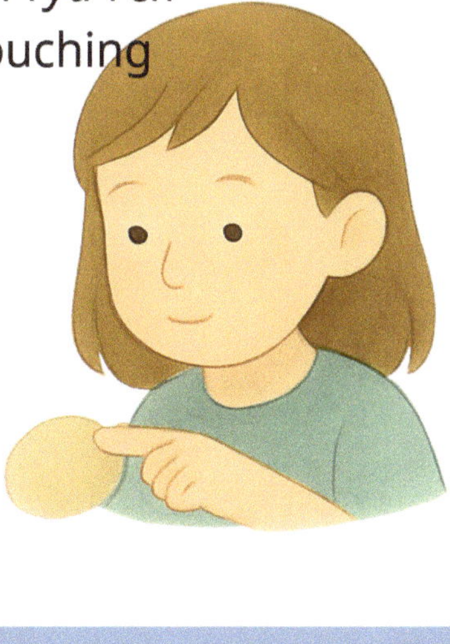

berühren
beh-ryu-ren
touching

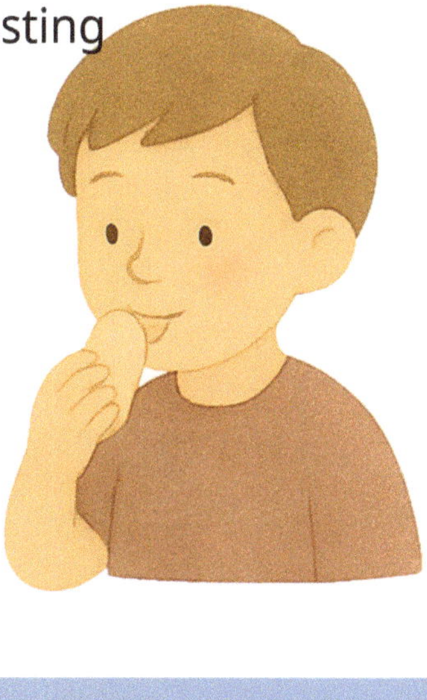

schmecken
shmek-ken
tasting

Emotions
Gefühle
geh-fyoo-leh

glücklich
glook-likh
happy

traurig
trow-rikh
sad

wütend
vyu-tent
angry

überrascht
oo-ber-rash-t
surprised

ängstlich
engst-likh
scared

aufgeregt
owf-geh-raygt
excited

My Body
Mein Körper
mine kur-per

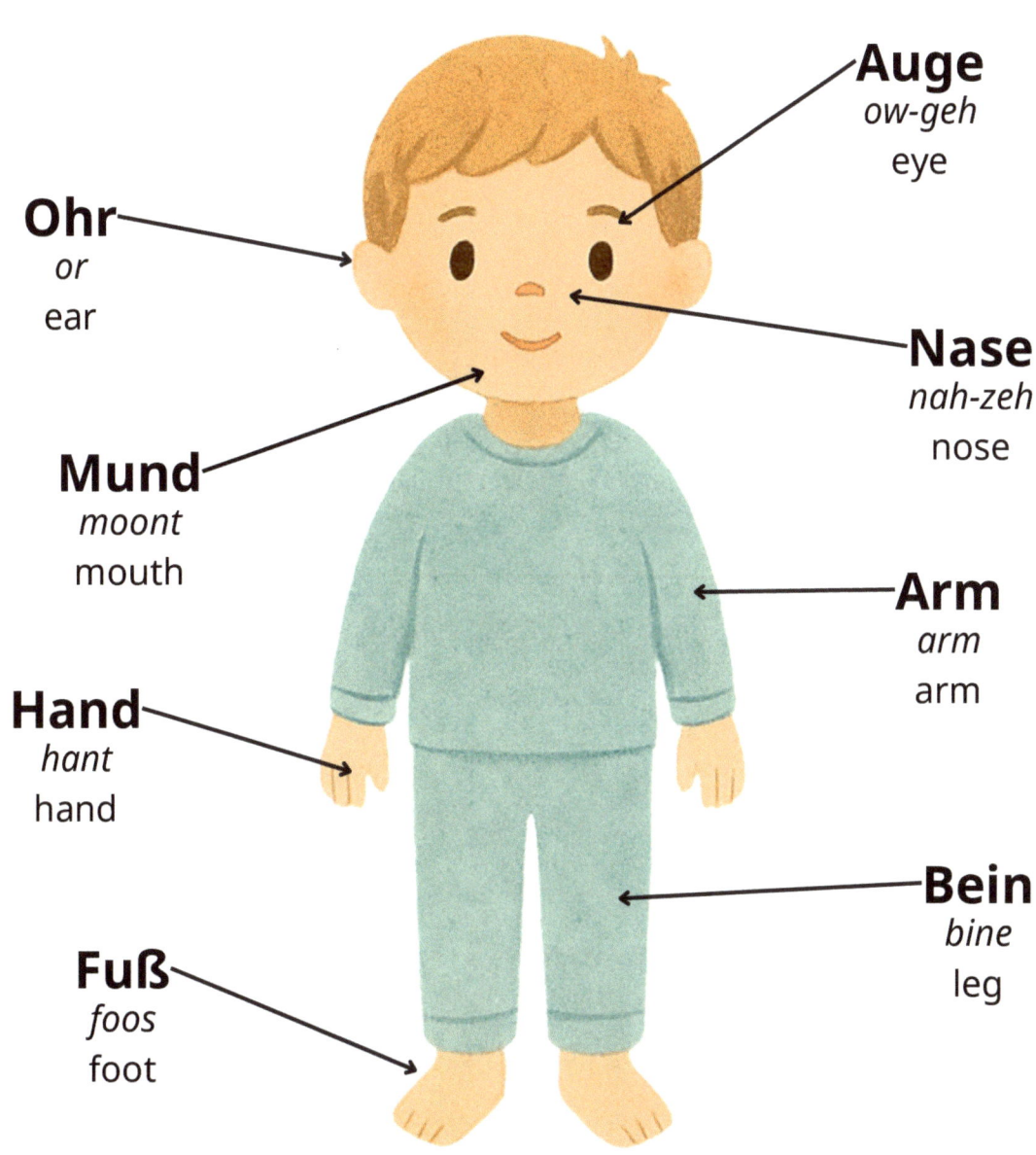

On The Washing Line

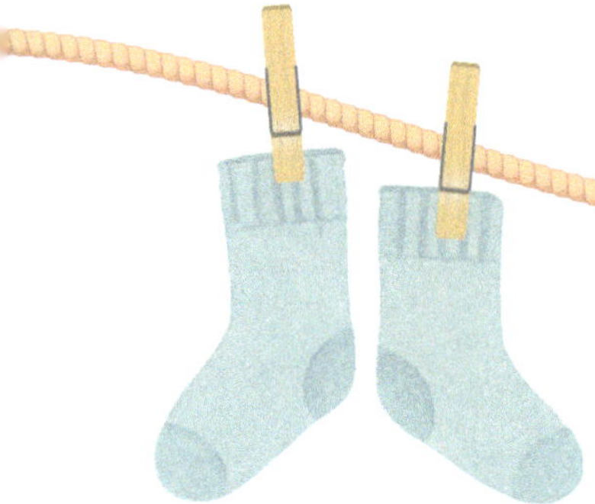

Socken
zo-ken
socks

Strumpfhose
shtroompf-ho-zeh
tights

T-Shirt
tee-shert
t-shirt

Mantel
man-tel
coat

Schuhe
shoo-eh
shoes

Rucksack
rook-sak
backpack

Food and Drink

Orange
oh-rang-geh
orange

Mais
mah-ees
sweetcorn

Trauben
trow-ben
grapes

Banane
bah-nah-neh
banana

Milch
milsh
milk

Cupcake
kup-kayk
cupcake

Inside the Shop
Im Geschäft
im geh-sheft

Einkaufswagen
ine-kowfs-vah-gen
trolley

Korb
korb
basket

Verkäufer
fer-koi-fer
shopkeeper

Geld
gelt
money

Kasse
kah-seh
till

Einkaufstasche
ine-kowfs-tah-sheh
shopping bag

Weather and Seasons

Sonnenschein
zon-en-shine
sunshine

Regen
reh-gen
rain

Wind
vint
wind

Wolken
vol-ken
clouds

Gewitter
geh-vit-ter
thunderstorm

Schnee
shnay
snow

Wetter und Jahreszeiten
veh-ter oont yah-res-tsy-ten

Sommer
zom-mer
summer

Frühling
froo-ling
spring

Herbst
herpst
autumn

Winter
vin-ter
winter

Numbers and Colours

1 **eins** *ines* one

2 **zwei** *tsvye* two

3 **drei** *dry* three

4 **vier** *feer* four

5 **fünf** *fuenf* five

6 **sechs** *zeks* six

7 **sieben** *zee-ben* seven

8 **acht** *ahẖt* eight

9 **neun** *noin* nine

10 **zehn** *tsayn* ten

Zahlen und Farben
tsah-len oont far-ben

Shapes
Formen
for-men

Kreis
krice
circle

Rechteck
rekh-tek
rectangle

Raute
rau-teh
rhombus

Herz
hertz
heart

Dreieck
dry-ike
triangle

Stern
shtern
star

Opposites
Gegensätze
gay-gen-zet-seh

kalt
kahlt
cold

heiß
hice
hot

groß
grohs
big

klein
kline
small

schnell
shnell
fast

langsam
long-zahm
slow

THANK YOU FOR CHOOSING THIS BOOK

IF YOU AND YOUR CHILD ENJOYED THIS BOOK, PLEASE CONSIDER LEAVING A REVIEW

REVIEWS HELP SMALL CREATORS LIKE US MAKE MORE BOOKS